T0207746

essentials

Springer essentials

Springer essentials provide up-to-date knowledge in a concentrated form. They aim to deliver the essence of what counts as "state-of-the-art" in the current academic discussion or in practice. With their quick, uncomplicated and comprehensible information, *essentials* provide:

- an introduction to a current issue within your field of expertise
- an introduction to a new topic of interest
- an insight, in order to be able to join in the discussion on a particular topic

Available in electronic and printed format, the books present expert knowledge from Springer specialist authors in a compact form. They are particularly suitable for use as eBooks on tablet PCs, eBook readers and smartphones. *Springer essentials* form modules of knowledge from the areas economics, social sciences and humanities, technology and natural sciences, as well as from medicine, psychology and health professions, written by renowned Springer-authors across many disciplines.

Astrid Polz-Watzenig

The Healing Effect
of the Forest
in Integrative Therapy

With Numerous Exercise Examples
for Practice

 Springer

Astrid Polz-Watzenig
psychotherapist (integrative therapy)
Graz, Austria

ISSN 2197-6708   ISSN 2197-6716   (electronic)
essentials
ISSN 2731-3107   ISSN 2731-3115   (electronic)
Springer essentials
ISBN 978-3-658-41642-3   ISBN 978-3-658-41643-0   (eBook)
https://doi.org/10.1007/978-3-658-41643-0

This Springer imprint is published by the registered company Springer Fachmedien Wiesbaden GmbH, part of Springer Nature.
The registered company address is: Abraham-Lincoln-Str. 46, 65189 Wiesbaden, Germany

What you can find in this *essential*

- What lies behind the experience of forest life
- How healing forest experience and integrative therapy work together
- How complex mindfulness can be developed
- How forest experience can be used in psychotherapeutic practice
- 14 exercise instructions for forest experience for psychotherapeutic practice and for self-care

Foreword

I am writing this foreword at a time when we in Austria are at the beginning of the third week of the Corona crisis, when Austria has been shut down to "emergency operation", and at a time when it is absolutely not yet foreseeable how long the drastic restrictions on social and economic life will have to last. In addition to the feeling of unreality and being diffusely threatened, the situation is not without a certain irony: a tiny organic structure—a virus—threatens to endanger the modern globalized culture of the most highly developed living being in its own assessment. This existential vulnerability of man, because he is inextricably part of nature, and at the same time his hubris to believe that he can gain absolute control over this nature, is evident in these developments, as well as a first glimpse of the possibility that the regenerative capacity of nature could be greater than previously assumed, if we only take the right measures as a globally networked and highly interdependent society. For example, air pollution has already decreased significantly in many places. How difficult it still seemed to anchor even approaches to effective measures against global warming in the turquoise-green government agreement, because this would not be economically justifiable. Now even the previously unthinkable must be possible, "whatever it costs", although not yet to save the climate, but to protect the people threatened by the virus in solidarity. But this current approach of politics shows what is possible in terms of social policy, when motivation and understanding, when emotional involvement and rational insight work together in a big enough way.

Everything feels is the programmatic title of a book by the biologist and philosopher Andreas Weber (2014), in which he passionately advocates complementing the objective approach to nature with the subjective perspective. Only from an intimate feeling of connectedness with nature can the urgently needed change in attitude arise, to no longer exploit it thoughtlessly, but to take responsibility and care for an intact nature together.

This passionate commitment is also consistently evident in the book at hand about the healing effect of the forest by Astrid Polz-Watzenig. In it, she examines how nature-therapeutic approaches can be described in detail through the various aspects of physicality, and how 14 intervention possibilities can then be implemented psychotherapeutically in a very concrete way. The author draws on her own experiences with breathing and mindfulness training as well as with the so-called Green Meditation according to Hilarion G. Petzold, without losing the necessary scientific distance. Psychotherapists who are looking for a scientific-based and practice-oriented approach to their nature-therapeutic considerations will greatly enjoy this book by Ms. Polz-Watzenig. In addition, it can be recommended to all people who are looking for suggestions on how to further deepen their own feeling of connection with nature, while at the same time receiving research-based information on how the healing effect of the forest is scientifically justified. I wish this book a large readership, especially in these difficult times.

Rosegg   Dr. Otto Hofer-Moser
on April, 2nd 2020   General practitioner
                                                  Training therapist for integrative therapy
                                                        at the Danube University Krems

Preface

Motivated by my training therapist Cornelia Cubasch-König, I completed the breathing and mindfulness teacher training with Peter Cubasch and the basic level of the Green Meditation training during my psychotherapy study. In doing so, the concept of complex mindfulness combined with the experience of the forest became a kind of nourishment for myself and my work.

Through the Nature Park Time-Out project, which I was able to accompany as a business consultant, I myself immersed deeper and deeper into the experience of the forest. I experienced how healing the experience of the forest can be—personally and in many accompaniments and encounters.

So the interest in the healing effect of the forest from the perspective of integrative therapy grew and eventually my master's thesis emerged, which serves as the basis for the book now at hand (Polz-Watzenig 2019).

My special thanks go to Dr. Otto Hofer-Moser for his prudent and committed support of my work and for his foreword, Eva Brechtl-Wahl and team for the support from the publisher.

I would also like to thank Claudia Gruber from the Nature Park Time-Out https://www.natura.at/de/NP-Auszeit/Naturpark-Auszeit and Katrin Heindl from www.pichlschloss.at for many inspiring moments and places.

Astrid Polz-Watzenig

Contents

1	**Introduction**	1
2	**Aspects of Experiencing the Forest**	3
	2.1 Ecological Aspects of Forest Experience	3
	2.2 Psychological Aspects of Experiencing the Forest	5
	2.3 Somatic Aspects of Experiencing the Forest	5
	2.4 Neuroscientifically Justified Effects of Experiencing the Forest: Facts and Studies	6
3	**Concepts of Health and Illness in Integrative Therapy**	9
	3.1 The Possible Significance of the Forest in Salutogenesis	9
4	**Anthropology of Integrative Therapy**	11
	4.1 The Anthropological Basic Axioms in Integrative Therapy	11
	4.2 Contemporary Phenomena of Alienation	12
	4.3 Integrative Eco-psychosomatics	13
5	**Aspects of Leiblichkeit**	15
	5.1 The Vertical Dimension	15
	5.2 The Horizontal Dimension	16
	5.3 The Concept of Intersubjectivity	17
	5.4 The Temporal Dimension	17
	5.5 The Social Body	18
6	**The Principle of Complex Mindfulness**	19
	6.1 Green Meditation (IGM)	19
	6.2 Forest Therapy	20
	6.3 Nature Therapies as an Important Addition to the Bundle of Possible Therapeutic Measures	20

**7   Specific Intervention forms for Experiencing the Forest
      from the Perspective of Complex Mindfulness**   23
      7.1   Experiencing the Forest in the Anamnesis   23

8   Complex Mindfulness in Experiencing the Forest—14 Exercises ...   27
      8.1   The Friendly Place   27
      8.2   Crossing the Threshold of the Forest into the Forest   28
      8.3   The "Worry Stone" Exercise at the Entrance to the Forest   28
      8.4   Going into the Forest with a Question   29
      8.5   Immersing Yourself in the Forest—with all Your Senses   29
      8.6   Exercise Three—Two—One   30
      8.7   Being Particularly Attracted by a Green   31
      8.8   Take a Closer Look   31
      8.9   The Walking Meditation Exercise   31
      8.10   The Roots in My Life   32
      8.11   Exiting the Forest   33
      8.12   The Journey Stick Exercise   34
      8.13   The Tree Exercise   34
      8.14   The Tree Exercise in Embodiment   35

9   The Forest on the Prescription   37
      9.1   The Forest in the Group Therapy Setting   39

10   Critical Reflection—Limitations   41

References   45

About the Author

Mag.ª Astrid Polz-Watzenig MSc, Psychotherapeutic practice, Schönaugasse 16, 8010 Graz, office@astridpolzwatzenig.at, www.astridpolzwatzenig.at

Introduction

If you take a look at the nature sections in bookstores today, the green almost grows towards you; forest bathing is on everyone's lips and a fashionable term. Numerous publications about the love of forests, trees and nature find countless buyers. This suggests that this trend is probably following a longing.

The question of the healing effect of the forest in integrative therapy is illuminated and answered from different perspectives in this book.

In the middle of the preparations for this book, the Covid-19 pandemic burst in and was suddenly omnipresent. In many ways, we experience this situation as a limitation of our horizon, as existentially threatening in the event of job loss, and as absolutely depressing in isolation, such as for the particularly vulnerable group of older people. Who would have thought that you could no longer simply decide freely where to travel, who to meet and how to spend your free time culturally, sportingly, socially. And the crisis will be with us for a long time to come.

In contrast, there is the experience of a spring, the awakening of nature, which is brought into focus precisely by the abolition of "everyday life" with all its accompanying phenomena of traffic, noise, and hustle and bustle, and, if you allow it, enchants more intensely than before. As a result, the intention of this book was unintentionally strengthened.

This book conveys the healing effect of the forest in integrative therapy both theoretically and practically. In addition to psychotherapists, this book can provide access to mindfulness and forest experience for all those who feel an increased longing for nature due to the current situation.

A. Polz-Watzenig, *The Healing Effect of the Forest in Integrative Therapy*, Springer essentials, https://doi.org/10.1007/978-3-658-41643-0_1

Aspects of Experiencing the Forest

2

What is good about staying in the forest can be clarified by illustrating the different aspects of forest life. In the context of integrative therapy, ecological, psychological, somatic and neuroscientific aspects are of particular interest.

2.1 Ecological Aspects of Forest Experience

When the word "ecology" is etymologically dissected, one comes across the ancient Greek words οἶκος, "oikos" and λόγος, "logos". οἶκος is translated as "dwelling house, house, apartment, single room, chamber, temple, cave or household, household, economy and ... permanent residence, homeland, fatherland" (Gemoll 1954, p. 534). λόγος also has several possible translations—"speaking", "teaching", "saying", "commands" or "prophecy", to name just a few (p. 475). As the word "household" already suggests, "ecology" is a comprehensive term—think of your own household or the household of a state.

Robert Macfarlane (2017) takes a look at the etymology of the word "forest".

> "The association of the wild and the wood also runs deep in etymology. The two words are thought to have grown out of the root word *wald* and the Old Teutonic root *walthus*, meaning 'forest'. *Walthus* entered Old English in its variant forms of 'weald', 'wald' and 'wold', which were used to designate both 'a wild place' and 'a wooded place', in which wild creatures — wolves, foxes, bears — survived. The wild and the wood also graft together in the latin word *silva*, which means 'forest', and from which emerged the idea of 'savage', with all its connotations of ferality" (p. 92).

Another—much more sober—definition of "forest" is provided by UNESCO, the United Nations Educational, Scientific and Cultural Organization. It defines it as follows: "A forest (forest) includes stands of trees with a height of more than 5

A. Polz-Watzenig, *The Healing Effect of the Forest in Integrative Therapy*, Springer essentials, https://doi.org/10.1007/978-3-658-41643-0_2

meters (in subpolar areas: 3 m, in the tropics: 8–10 m), whose canopy is closed" (Greiner and Kiem 2019, p. 13).

When heat waves increase in Austria, spruce monocultures fall victim to bark beetle infestation, forest fires are no longer containable and increasing storm and hail damage threatens the entire forest stock, it becomes apparent that the forest is in serious danger today. It is hard to imagine that there were also times without forests (cf. pp. 36–37). "Although during Roman times (about 400 BC to 500 AD) Germania was described above all as the land of the endless, dark and eerie primeval forests, the forest area in Europe was already cleared by a third at that time" (pp. 36–37). After the discovery of America, entire forest areas fell victim to shipbuilding due to Spain's expansion drive—Greiner and Kiem speak of the first energy crisis, which took place around 1500, and call it "wood shortage".

Peter Wohlleben also illustrates the ecological disasters the forest experienced in his book "*The Forest: A Journey of Discovery*", which was published in 2016. The depictions of the romanticism of the painter Casper David Friedrich are familiar—with individual trees in a barren landscape, they exude a deep melancholy. According to Wohlleben, these images refer to a lost idyll, as by the middle of the nineteenth century the last primeval forest in Europe had already been cleared.

The barrenness, the lack, the loss, which are illustrated in the pictures by Caspar David Friedrich, such as in the picture "The Woman with the Spider Web between Bare Trees", are also reflected in the following quote:

> We have a tendency to pity and glorify dying creatures. Whether it is oppressed peoples like the indigenous people of North America or the last blue whales, many of us feel deep compassion and awe. And this was also given to the remaining trees. The lost natural idyll of untouched forests was glorified and anchored in our souls until today. With positive consequences, because with the end of the Romantic era the forest began to expand again. (Wohlleben 2016, p. 44)

Not only the construction of ships demanded wood, but also for the production of iron, charcoal was increasingly needed in huge quantities. At the beginning of the twentieth century, among other things, the two world wars led to deforestation and clear-cutting. The German word "Waldsterben" was borrowed into English and the years after 1945 are referred to as "locust years" (see Macfarlane 2017, pp. 97–100).

2.2   Psychological Aspects of Experiencing the Forest

Robert Macfarlane emphasizes in *The Wild Places* (2017) the importance of the forest for human imagination, for fairy tales and stories, but also especially for the mind and spirit. "Woods, like other ild places, can kindle new ways of being or cognition in people, can urge their minds differently" (p. 98–99). He also writes about the Persian king Xerxes, "… who so loved sycamores that, when marching to war with the Greeks, he halted his army of many thousands of men in order that they might contemplate and admire one outstanding specimen" (p. 99). The French writer and aviator Antoine de Saint-Exupéry writes in 1933 about his arrival in the jungle of Senegal after a flight with Libyan tribal leaders from their desert: "… they 'wept at the sight of the trees', never having encountered such beings before" (p. 100).

This reaction makes it clear what power can lie in the *greening of the soul*—a term coined by Hilarion Petzold. "**Green** is a 'color metaphor' for vitality, health, growth, life force, hope, the 'green side' of young love, and **green** is more than that: it is the existential feeling of life, …" (Petzold 2015, p. 2)

Li (2019), known in our latitudes as *the* founder and representative of Shinrin Yoku—the Japanese term for forest bathing—investigated psychological reactions of women and men with Profile-of-Mood-States tests. It turned out that "… forest bathing … significantly reduces the values for tension, depression, irritability, fatigue and confusion and significantly increases the value for vigor …" (p. 279), and Li was able to further identify a particular effectiveness "in psychological stress (mental exhaustion)" (p. 279).

2.3   Somatic Aspects of Experiencing the Forest

Li (2018) already notes physiologically positive aspects after just a two-hour stay in the forest. This requires a willingness to slow down and engage in order to live in the moment and relax. When you immerse yourself in nature with all five senses, you begin to reap the many benefits it offers. There is now a large amount of data showing what Shinrin Yoku can offer (p. 38):

- "Reduce blood pressure
- Lower stress
- Improve cardiovascularand metabolic health
- Lower blood-sugar levels
- Improve concentration and memory

- Lift depression
- Improve pain thresholds
- Improve energy
- Boosts the immune system with an increase in the count of the body's natural killer cells (NK) cells
- Increase anti-cancer protein production
- Help you to lose weigh"

2.4   Neuroscientifically Justified Effects of Experiencing the Forest: Facts and Studies

The immune system was long considered independently of the human nervous or hormonal system, but it is now generally accepted that "… the activation of peripheral immune cells leads to changes in brain function. Conversely, the activation of certain brain nerve cells leads to immunoregulatory, neuroendocrine reactions" (Li 2019, p. 275).

Stress control in the human body is carried out by the autonomic nervous system. The activating sympathetic nervous system and the relaxing parasympathetic nervous system, "referred to in medicine as 'vagus' for short, after its largest nerve" (Moser and Thoma 2014, p. 119), are in opposition to each other. The basis for a successful balance, i.e. an equilibrium of vagus and sympathetic nervous system, is the enzyme balance of acetylcholine—which is released during relaxation—and acetylcholinesterase, i.e. the breakdown of acetylcholine during tension. Studies have found that pinenes—*essential* active ingredients contained in conifers—"… effectively inhibit the stress-inducing acetylcholinesterase and protect the calming vagus substance from being destroyed too quickly" (p. 120).

In this context, Moser and Thoma refer to the fact that the vagus also has another important function in connection with stopping inflammatory reactions in the body. "In fact, studies have shown that tree resin ingredients have a strong anti-inflammatory effect. Interestingly, these substances have an anti-inflammatory effect mainly when they combine with atmospheric oxygen" (p. 120).

The use of plants that contain alpha-pinene also brings about an "amazing regeneration of beta cells in the Langerhans's islands" (p. 121) and leads to a reduction in glycated hemoglobin, which can explain possible positive effects for people with diabetes.

The positive effect of pinenes is also mentioned in connection with the prevention of osteoporosis, as they can also inhibit the formation of bone-degrading cells.

Another effect is said to be a certain anti-cancer effect. Plants have protective mechanisms that protect them from proliferations, such as the turpentine oil of the Swiss pine, spruce or larch (see pp. 118–119). Transferring this effect to humans would be desirable, but studies to substantiate this are still lacking.

The pinenes already mentioned reach the limbic system directly via the olfactory receptors, which is responsible for controlling our emotions. People communicate with each other not least through smells (pheromones). "Fear, sexual accessibility as well as sexual rejection, but also dominance and other behaviors are often sniffed out between people. Without saying a word about it" (p. 116).

The technical term for the secondary plant substances, such as the already mentioned alpha and beta pinenes, is "phytoncides", which belong to the group of terpenes. They are produced by plants and trees in the forest and are present in different concentrations in the forest air. When someone is out in the forest, these substances can be absorbed through the lungs.

The journal *Nature* published the results of a study involving 91,190 people of all ages in May 2019 with the title "Spending at least 120 min a week in nature is associated with good health and wellbeing" by White et al. and found out:

"A two-hour 'dose' of nature a week significantly boosts health and wellbeing, research suggests, even if you simply sit and enjoy the peace" (Carrington 2019, p. 1).

Concepts of Health and Illness in Integrative Therapy

3

In integrative therapy, health and illness are seen as two poles of a continuum, which makes it clear that they are in a dialectical relationship.

Petzold (2003) distinguishes between a general or anthropological theory of illness ("illness is based on dysregulation and alienation") and an anthropological theory of health ("health is based on integrity, coherence and belonging") (p. 447).

Illness and health are linked to a developmental process. With regard to the concept of health, Petzold refers to the concept of salutogenesis by Aaron Antonovsky, an Israeli-American stress researcher and medical sociologist, who developed this concept as a counterpoint to the pathogenesis concept. "Salutogenesis" is often referred to as "genesis of health"—Greiner and Kiem (2019) also adopt this translation in German based on the Latin "salus" (health) and the ancient Greek "genesis".

"Whoever understands how to shape their own life, give their life meaning and keep everything in balance, experiences a feeling of coherence and stays healthy longer" (p. 24).

3.1 The Possible Significance of the Forest in Salutogenesis

What risk factors and what protective factors surround us? Over the lifespan, a forest has always been a place of refuge, peace, recreation, intimacy or solitude. Co-creatively and constructively, physical, emotional, mental and social as well as ecological potentials can be developed (see Ellerbrock and Petzold 2019, p. 745). This means that maintaining health is subject to a process of emergence; new

A. Polz-Watzenig, *The Healing Effect of the Forest in Integrative Therapy*, Springer essentials, https://doi.org/10.1007/978-3-658-41643-0_3

things can be tried and learned, and regular "forest experiences" can thus become an *essential* factor in maintaining health.

One factor that also seems worth mentioning in connection with this is the relationship between the forest and social health. Feelings of social "non-belonging" are hardly ever triggered in the forest, unlike in urban spaces (pp. 748–749). Forest and park landscapes are especially important places for social interaction and integration for young people and children of "any social and cultural background", while for adults who consciously seek out nature, they "like to go to the forest alone, like to be alone with themselves in the forest, are quiet, enjoy the silence" (p. 749).

Anthropology of Integrative Therapy

Which anthropology does the Integrative Therapy represent? How does the disturbance occur, or, to use the technical term, the alienation from the body, from the environment, etc.?

4.1 The Anthropological Basic Axioms in Integrative Therapy

The image of man in Integrative Therapy defines man intersubjectively, as co-creative with one another, creative in the context of life and in lifetime (in context and continuum). "Expressed in the language of philosophy, man is a 'body subject in the life world'—or, put differently: 'man is as man and woman a body-soul-spirit-being in a social and ecological environment, in a concrete, historical time'" (Krüskemper 2019, p. 618).

As a body subject, man needs the You, which also makes him an I. Through the We of several body subjects, a community is created. "Man is not être dans le monde, but être-au-monde …" (Petzold 2003, p. 409) and is characterized by both uniqueness and plurality. And both, the uniqueness as well as the diversity, are endangered by "isolation, alienation, colonization, self-reification" (p. 409).

In the context of the anthropological theory of disease in Integrative Therapy, the concept of multiple alienation is found. Petzold uses and emphasizes the concept of alienation from Marx's and Hegel's philosophy by expanding it through social-philosophical as well as existential and body-philosophical perspectives. "The multiple alienation of man includes, among other things, the alienation from one's own body, from fellow human beings, from the life world, from work and from time" (Leitner 2010, p. 167). In the context of the question at hand,

A. Polz-Watzenig, *The Healing Effect of the Forest in Integrative Therapy*, Springer essentials, https://doi.org/10.1007/978-3-658-41643-0_4

it is important to take a closer look at contemporary phenomena of alienation, especially with regard to an ecological perspective.

4.2   Contemporary Phenomena of Alienation

Wolfgang Lalouschek, specialist in neurology and coach as well as burnout specialist, said in a lecture in April 2019 that people usually do not question their communication behavior. Every time you check your phone for a message, your brain activates a variety of activities. If you transfer this communication behavior to the times before the smartphone, it would be as if someone was checking their mailbox every few minutes.

In an interview with the daily newspaper *Der Standard*, Lalouschek summarizes the consequences of this constant distraction:

> The constant distraction by digital media has an effect on our brain, because even in our free time there are suddenly no more rest periods. Anyone who is constantly online deprives their brain of the vital rest periods. Because social media is only seemingly free time, for the brain it is stress, as measurements clearly show. Under stress, the limbic system in the brain is active. It is the functional unit responsible for processing emotions. Fear and insecurity are strong emotions that are constantly brought to consciousness by constant multitasking. That is why many younger people also have a permanent latent fear. (Pollack 2019)

Another example: Can buildings make you sick? Greiner and Kiem (2019) describe the so-called Sick Building Syndrome (SBS). People who are always at the same workplace inside a building can suffer from things like "teary eyes, … skin irritations, cough, cold, taste and smell disorders, discomfort, headaches, concentration problems or exhaustion" (p. 18). The special thing about it is that these symptoms disappear after work or after leaving the building and work context.

A third example is described by Daniela Haluza (2019), who quotes the American author and journalist Richard Louv, who links the lack of nature experience in children and adolescents with the increase in diseases such as obesity, attention deficit hyperactivity disorder (ADHD) or depression in childhood and adolescence. Louv "… coined the term 'nature deficit syndrome' for this, which is not to be understood as a disease, but as a phenomenon of increasing alienation from nature, which is characteristic of the modern post-industrial society" (p. 15).

4.3   Integrative Eco-psychosomatics

The therapist's gaze is always directed at the body, which is to be seen contextualized with its embedding. Negative embodiments are negative traces in the body left by negative environmental influences and present/stored in the interoceptive memory. "The **internalization** of positive environmental impressions through **'corrective ecological experiences'** can and must change this" (Petzold and Hömberg 2019, pp. 264–265).

What is required, therefore, is an integrative eco-psychosomatics. This is based on "the concept of the 'informed body, the informing environment' and the living, global context of 'living together' (i.e. mundane conviviality). Exclusions, 'ecological deprivation' (nature deficit) and aggressive threats (nature destruction) therefore have a stress-inducing effect" (pp. 264–265). This can be transferred to all living beings, with the area of mass animal husbandry to be mentioned as well as the negative effects of open-plan offices.

Aspects of Leiblichkeit

5

As has already become clear, a very central concept of integrative therapy is the "Leib" concept (body concept). Based on this, it is important to develop an understanding of human existence and "… the 'essence' of being human as a *body-soul-spirit-whole* and its *to-and-in-the-world-being* …" (Hofer-Moser 2018, p. 11). Basic concepts of integrative therapy, such as intersubjectivity, intercorporeality and living environment, are based on this. When body-oriented and body-centered interventions are now linked to forest experiences, the terminology in relation to body experience must first be defined along the body concept of integrative therapy.

5.1 The Vertical Dimension

"The vertical dimension encompasses … the entire range from the 'functioning' to the 'subjectively feeling' and 'affectively affected' to the 'reflective body' in fully developed eccentricity" (Hofer-Moser 2018, p. 44).

The "self-body awareness" brings the feeling into play: "Feelings are spatial, but locationless, poured out atmospheres" (Schmitz 2015, p. 23). Schmitz clarifies using the example of a feeling of silence that it is about the feeling of tightness and width. "A solemn or a delicate morning silence is wide, while a pressing, burdensome, leaden silence is tight and protopathically dull" (p. 23).

Taking a forest clearing as an example of a perception exercise, some people will perceive the immersion in the forest as quiet, refreshing, and shade-giving and will be able to enjoy it. Others, on the other hand, will perceive the buzzing insects, the darkness, the screeching call of the crows as discomfort and feel tension and tightness.

A. Polz-Watzenig, *The Healing Effect of the Forest in Integrative Therapy*, Springer essentials, https://doi.org/10.1007/978-3-658-41643-0_5

The perception here is less focused on the skin as an outer boundary, but rather a dynamic of tightness and width is experienced through breathing. The feeling can be holistic or limited to parts of so-called "Leibinseln" (body islands)

This differentiating self-body sensing requires practice; mindfulness exercises in the forest can be a way to work on this sensing in more depth.

5.2   The Horizontal Dimension

The horizontal dimension encompasses the sensory body or the situational body, both of which are parts of the perceptive body. The perceptive body informs on the one hand through interoceptors about its "internal state", i.e. about the state of individual organs and organ systems, and on the other hand about the "functional state" of the organism as a whole. "The interoceptors include the enteroceptors and the immunoreceptors … as well as the proprioceptors" (Hofer-Moser 2018, p. 46). Proprioception and the sense of balance are involved in the "feeling of being situationally embedded". Through the exteroceptors "… the integration/embedding of the body in its living environment is realized even further" (p. 46). The enteroceptors provide feedback to the organs, for example, about the feeling of hunger or an "uncomfortable gut feeling" that can occur when a socially influenced situation turns out to be tense or difficult.

Thermoreceptors and nociceptors inform about body states internally, just as the near sense informs about the exterior (e.g. about how hot it is outside). "All these signals from the interoceptors are related to each other in the 'insula cortex', a part of the cerebral cortex …, and thus form the basis of the emerging body-self or—together with the information from the immune system …—the basis of our own bodily awareness" (p. 47).

This bodily awareness seems to be responsible for our sense of time as well, for example, when we think of meditation experiences.

The actual horizontal dimension begins where the body knows about its immediate environment through the exteroceptors—for example, by touching, tasting, smelling, seeing or hearing. These "percepts" connect to previous experiences, which in turn connect to an implicit temporal dimension. It is about relating to the "memorative body" …, to our current inner drives, needs, motivations and to our creative-creative impulses" (p. 50). Thus, through the impulses endowed with meaning and significance, the "informed body" ultimately emerges, which "… as an 'expressive body' with its many individual verbal and non-verbal expression, design and coping possibilities, comes to a corresponding response and/or a new inquiry to the living environment" (p. 50).

Integrative therapy speaks of the situational body, which is embedded in the living environment through "bodily communication". "The 'personal body subject' is understood as existentially 'embedded', 'woven in', 'embedded' in its relevant socio-ecological context against the background of a lifelong development process" (p. 52–53).

5.3   The Concept of Intersubjectivity

From infancy, we have learned that our body allows us to imitate "*essential others*" up to the point of model learning through conscious and unconscious imitation. This is the "ability of the body" to expand into a "… 'total sensory organ'—also including the neurobiological concept of the so-called mirror neuron systems—to the ability of a 'total resonance organ' …" (Hofer-Moser 2018, p. 57).

Through our "resonant body" we find "… more or less access to the inner perspective of other people in terms of empathy, as one, but not the exclusive basis for lived intersubjectivity and compassion" (p. 57).

This view can be extended to nature, and so "one comes to a concept of **Naturempathie** (nature empathy), in which nature must also be experienced bodily-concretely 'outdoor', as it were 'intersubjectively'" (Petzold and Orth-Petzold 2019, p. 363).

5.4   The Temporal Dimension

The temporal dimension encompasses our memory systems. In integrative therapy, a distinction is made between explicit and implicit memory. Explicit memory is conscious, so-called biographically nourished, declared memory, a fact memory, a "knowing that". Implicit memory, the body memory or the "knowing how", is formed unconsciously. Here one can distinguish between procedural, situational, intersubjective and incorporated memory (cf. Hofer-Moser 2018, p. 60).

The direction of explicit memory goes from the present to the past. The person verbalizes and recalls biographical scenes or has factual knowledge. "Implicit memory, on the other hand, does not recall the past, but contains it as an experience that is effective in the present. … One could say that in remembering we *have* our past, while in the bodily experience of life we *are* our past" (Fuchs 2008; quoted in Hofer-Moser 2018, p. 61).

5.5   The Social Body

It makes a difference whether someone was born into a small village community in the countryside and grew up surrounded by forests, meadows and familiar people, or in an urban environment, anonymously, in the concrete jungle. "With the concept of a 'social body', the importance of the dynamic embedding of people in their relevant socio-cultural background—from conception onwards, … in the sense of a continuous socialization and enculturation process—is taken into account" (Hofer-Moser 2018, p. 62).

In a socio-cultural context in the ecological sense, the question arises of experiencing nature in one's own life and in that of the people with whom one is on their life journey.

It makes a difference whether a mindful approach to one's own person and the environment was demonstrated, whether this is foreign to someone, or whether this can be a desirable path for the individual in question, in the sense of a corrective experience.

The Principle of Complex Mindfulness

"Complex mindfulness must be directed towards the **body** and the **life environment**. One cannot understand, possess, or intervene in one without the other" (Petzold et al. 2019, p. 232). Ultimately, the goal of such development is "euthymic mindfulness", i.e. a sensitivity to one's "own well-being" and the "well-being of others" (p. 232).

Such mindfulness requires resonance capability and the alertness of the person, as well as continuous development in the practice of becoming complexly mindful. "In it, one *ponders*—about the state of nature. One *senses* when one hears news of ecological destruction or disasters that have affected people. We make ourselves mindful and touchable here" (p. 234).

6.1 Green Meditation (IGM)

"In **IGM**—and ultimately in most forms of meditation—the starting point is one's own **"body"**. It is the foundation and the beginning—and with the view of one's own death, it is also the end of any meditative practice. The living body with its *neuroplastic* brain, the basis of the body subject, which is embedded in the world with its personality developed over the "lifespan", becomes the place of practice, preferably in "green places of nature" or with imaginary green images" (Petzold et al. 2019, p. 51 f.).

By practicing on the three levels of meditation—contemplation, observation, and immersion—a complex mindfulness sets in for the meditator, which "brings about relaxation, destressing, and promotes serenity, inner peace, and personal sovereignty" (p. 52).

Especially in the experience of the forest, Green Meditation offers a versatile opportunity.

A. Polz-Watzenig, *The Healing Effect of the Forest in Integrative Therapy*, Springer essentials, https://doi.org/10.1007/978-3-658-41643-0_6

6.2   Forest Therapy

As part of the new nature therapies, Petzold, Hömberg and Ellerbrock (2019) also defined forest therapy: "Forest therapy aims to use the life and ecosystem 'forest' as a health-promoting and healing experience space, guided and accompanied by professionally trained experts (forest therapists, forest health advisors)" (p. 47).

But forest therapy is also used in a multi-professional manner to treat pathogenic conditions—psychosomatic and psychological disorders. The field of application is broad, and the methods can be used as important components of "… a 'forest medicine', 'ecopsychosomatics' and 'clinical ecology' in the context of complex therapy programs with multimodal bundles of therapeutic measures" (p. 47).

What is special about forest therapy, about working with the forest experience, is that the ecological imperative—"Take care not to harm nature!"—is demanded here. In the love of the forest, everything is included: the "care for nature as 'caring for nature, eco-care', … an 'ecosophy', as well as a love for the living, a love for the forest—an 'ecophilia' as 'caring for life, caring for people'." This also includes mindful self-care (self caring), because humans are part of nature" (p. 47).

6.3   Nature Therapies as an Important Addition to the Bundle of Possible Therapeutic Measures

In integrative therapy, 14 healing factors, also called effective factors or processes, are formulated: empathetic understanding (EV), emotional acceptance and support (ES), help with practical life management/life help (LH), promotion of emotional expression and volitional decision-making power (EA), promotion of insight, experience of meaning, experience of evidence (EE), promotion of communicative skills and relationship skills (KK), promotion of physical awareness, self-regulation and psychophysical relaxation (LB), promotion of learning opportunities, learning processes and interests (LM), promotion of creative experience opportunities and creative forces (KG), development of positive future perspectives (PZ), promotion of a positive, personal value reference (PW), promotion of a distinctive self and identity experience, sovereignty (PI), promotion of sustainable social networks (TN), enabling of experiences of solidarity and solid partnerships (SE) (see Krüskemper 2019, pp. 624–628).

In 2016, these 14 healing factors were supplemented by three more, which are particularly important in the context of the new nature therapy.

a) **Promotion of a lively and regular connection to nature (NB):**

Petzold et al. (2016) point out that the meta-factor of an undamaged and unburdened ecology is an important specific effective factor, especially when "… negative effects are observed in patients due to the lack of connections to nature" (p. 30).

In this context, Petzold refers to Louv's "Nature Deficit Syndrome" or speaks of "Nature Deficit Disorders"—but both are not clinical diagnoses in the sense of an ICD-10 diagnosis. Especially with children and adolescents who have no experience of nature, it becomes clear what developmental moment is missing, which makes this factor of influence a necessity. An "engagement for nature" can also have a healing effect here.

Four principles are important in the context of this "pro-nature attitude" and an ecologically appropriate lifestyle (see p. 30):

- a **"concern for the living (eco-caring, caring for nature)",** because it is endangered,
- the **"loving care for the living ("ecophilia")",** because this living is valuable,
- **"complex responsibility for the diversity of the living"** and
- **"joy in the living",** because living nature is enriching, enlightening, inspiring and again and again beautiful and fulfilling for people.

These four principles justify for Petzold a new, nature- and world-related **"art of living".** As such, they also establish the connection to the next healing and influencing factor.

b) **Mediation of healing aesthetic experiences (AE):**

Many people know the feeling that a particularly beautiful tree in a forest clearing evokes with its sublimity and that it touches you with its beauty. Or that a piece of music, a poem, a work of visual art moves you deeply. "Beauty—of nature, music, poetry, painting—has a constructive healing power, whether through receptive reception or through creative design, in which one enjoys the aesthetics" (Petzold et al. 2016, p. 31).

c) **Synergetic multimodality (SM):**

The Integrative Therapy was never monocausal in its etiology; there are "causes behind the causes" and "consequences behind the consequences". This

multifactoriality was thus already given. But this 17th healing and active factor speaks to the fact that efforts to understand by patients, therapists, are
phenomenologically-hermeneutically multi-perspective and should be supplemented or "flanked" by other process facilitators (e.g. from areas of social
work, physiotherapy, movement therapy, creative therapy, nature therapy, etc.).
It is these insights gained in these areas that, in addition to the therapist's
own insights from the "bundle of measures", can contribute significantly to
promoting the health efforts of patients. This happens located in their social
convoys of family, friends, and supports the change of dysfunctional lifestyles
(see Petzold et al. 2016, p. 31).

Specific Intervention forms for Experiencing the Forest from the Perspective of Complex Mindfulness

7

Experiencing the forest brings with it positive aspects. In order to experience these, it is necessary to "come into contact" with them. It is never too late—especially in terms of corrective ecological experiences—to catch up on what has not been experienced and to learn or to reactivate and deepen what has already been experienced. A first step can be to specifically inquire about this topic as part of the anamnesis.

7.1 Experiencing the Forest in the Anamnesis

"When we go about asking for 'the story' in psychotherapeutic anamneses, we have to ask: What is experienced history? What is narrated history? And: What influence does the interviewer have on the content and manner of presentation of this story?" (Osten 2000, p. 33). In Integrative Therapy, there is the approach of "discursive-narrative" hermeneutics in order to understand intersubjectively narrated stories, which is linked to "dramatic-actional" hermeneutics, the "narrative practice". Identity, illness, are shaped in relationand in relation to other people, in "co-actions", i.e. as a response to actions. In the process, "stories" emerge. These are cognitively and physically—as well as stories of health maintenance—quasi archived in the body memory (cf. p. 33).

The act of storytelling itself becomes an intervention, as does the therapist's listening and responding.

Anamnesis can thus be understood as an entry point into the work of remembering and growing a narrated—but also an un-narrated—story.

The question arises here as to what a co-action with the ecological environment or a reflection of it might look like. It is generally assumed that all

A. Polz-Watzenig, *The Healing Effect of the Forest in Integrative Therapy*, Springer essentials, https://doi.org/10.1007/978-3-658-41643-0_7

patients are aware of their ecological bodily experience. The question now is how (strongly) this can be brought into consciousness.

When asked about the place of early childhood, one can also ask whether access to nature was available. Was there a forest nearby? Did the person play in the forest? Were there favorite trees, tree houses, hiding places? What memories are there of the forest in childhood? People from socially disadvantaged backgrounds often do not have the resources for varied leisure activities. Admission to the swimming pool, skiing in winter—all this and more is associated with costs. But access to the forest is—in European latitudes—almost always possible free of charge.

Were trips to the forest made in kindergarten? Perhaps materials were collected and then arranged into mandalas, perhaps forest spirit games were invented or knight fights were fought with self-found sticks.

Some people are afraid of insects, while others are full of amazement at their diversity and beauty. This behavior often has its origins in childhood. Were there perhaps discoveries in the humus of the forest? For some, a frog may have been an enchanted fairy tale prince and thus became part of the narrated stories. Perhaps worms were examined particularly closely or woodlice races were held. It makes a difference whether accompanying adults are disgusted or do not allow getting dirty or even associate it with scolding.

It is fascinating that children in the forest don't need any utensils or things to start playing. They can follow their imagination in the prevailing situation and develop exciting games. When they are given space to move, they climb, run, jump, and poke around in puddles. They observe insects, and maybe even collect them. The sounds of the forest can be experienced intensely or even imitated with pleasure.

These examples—easy to supplement across all ages—are meant to show how the ecological perspective is automatically included in the biographical anamnesis by asking when and where the forest was important. In addition, this also allows for an additional focus on the important resource work in the therapeutic process from the outset.

Possibility of application in life panorama work in the therapeutic setting
In integrative therapy, the "panorama technique" is sometimes used as a diagnostic tool in the current life span. This method makes it possible to gain a broader and more accurate overview (see Petzold 2003, p. 993).

The panorama technique can be used in different ways; for example, as a complete life panorama, as a health/illness panorama, or, with a modified question, focused on a particular aspect.

In the classic life panorama, patients are invited to present the "chains of adverse and 'critical life events'" that represent risk factors. At the same time, they are also asked to present the "chains of salutogenic influences, the protective factors." Ultimately, it is also about identifying experiences of lack, which usually occur in the context of the respective relationship experiences (see p. 993). Setting an ecological focus here, investigating forest and nature experiences, can be particularly rewarding in the context of resource work. The favorite tree from childhood can be rediscovered, and negative forest experiences can also be included in the therapeutic work.

A specific question could be worded as follows:

- In which places in nature have you felt particularly good, happy, and secure?
- What influence did the forest experience have in these moments?
- Do you remember the feeling in your body? What smells, sounds, and moods do you remember?
- How do you feel now when you think of these memories; what do you feel now?

Pillars of identity

Another tool for anamnesis is the five pillars of identity. With the help of these, a quick overview of the current stability of the patient can be obtained. Petzold defined these five pillars (see Petzold 2003, p. 775):

- "Leiblichkeit" (Body, Embodiment) /
- Social network
- Work and performance
- Material security
- Values

In connection with these five pillars, the question of experiencing the forest in particular and/or experiencing nature in general can be asked on several levels; first in the context of "Leiblichkeit". This often already addresses how one feels where, e.g. in nature, or which diet is preferred. In the area of social networks, the forest can play a big role due to the presence of like-minded people. In the area of values, it is also an important question what view someone has of nature, what belief or ethical attitude is behind it—a wide range of values is available.

There are people for whom all five pillars are damaged, but even for them, the connection to nature can sometimes help, because nature is equally present for everyone, the forest is also accessible for those who cannot afford anything, have no work and whose body is impaired. The importance of this availability is particularly evident in the current Corona crisis.

Complex Mindfulness in Experiencing the Forest—14 Exercises

8

These 14 exercises have all been practiced by myself and are therefore reproduced accordingly. Some of them were developed by myself and some were taken from the literature presented.

8.1 The Friendly Place

As part of the Green Meditation training, you are asked on the first weekend to find a place that you should visit again and again now and throughout the entire training, which will take several years—three times a day during the first training weekend, the timing is left to the learner.

This place in the forest or on the edge of the forest is consciously and slowly selected at the beginning and you have about an hour to do so.

Regardless of whether you are lying, sitting, or standing, the task is initially to fully grasp this place. This grasping happens through the senses—what you see, smell, hear, taste, touch. You have an empty book and a pen with you, and you should record and write down what comes to mind.

Over time, this place becomes a place for conversation, inner dialogue, and exchange. Sometimes it is fresh and airy, sometimes stuffy and oppressive, and it is also about noticing these differences. Sometimes the place is full of life, birds, beetles, worms—for example after a rain shower in summer, everything steams and is full of excitement and movement. Another time this is not or hardly the case. It is important to notice these differences, intercorporeally, in "nature empathy". The perception in the sense of complex mindfulness reveals that relaxation sets in through the slowing down of breathing. Tensions in the muscles may dissolve, a yawn may occur, which in turn promotes relaxation. By focusing on the place, it becomes possible to perceive that there is nothing

A. Polz-Watzenig, *The Healing Effect of the Forest in Integrative Therapy*,
Springer essentials, https://doi.org/10.1007/978-3-658-41643-0_8

else right now. Thoughts about work, home, or tomorrow are absent. If they do appear, they can be kindly asked to move on.

The smells are also absorbed through breathing—how do they change over the course of the day, the seasons?

One way to anchor these feelings in everyday life is to take a little something from this special place, such as a leaf, a stone, a piece of wood—as a reminder of the return and as a "bookmark".

8.2   Crossing the Threshold of the Forest into the Forest

Essential for this exercise is a good arrival, a being here, an attentiveness in feeling the rooting through one's own legs on the ground.

There is no quick "starting into the forest", but rather a "going to the edge of the forest". There it is then about crossing the threshold, every forest offers such entrance portals, if one pays attention to it. Before entering, everyone makes themselves aware of what should be left behind at the threshold, what wants to be put down, as if one were putting down a heavy backpack. This putting down and stripping off is supported by physical exercises.

First, attention is paid to a good stance, the breathing is consciously perceived. The shoulders are raised, moved backwards in a circular motion, the shoulder blades are brought together so that they touch. With an intensified exhalation, the imagined backpack is put down. Through this exercise, participants often realize for the first time how tense their breathing has been so far. By consciously inhaling, "putting down the backpack", the flow of breath changes, is perceived differently, the facial features relax.

Silence is of condensing importance in this exercise and should be particularly motivated in the instructions.

8.3   The "Worry Stone" Exercise at the Entrance to the Forest

This exercise is an opportunity to free oneself from unnecessary mental baggage, the wandering mind. It invites you to look for a stone at the edge of the forest. This should be done without any specifications regarding the size or nature of the stone. This stone is examined, "grasped", receives full attention. Finally, the stone is touched and the thought burdening the forest walk is deposited with the stone. "Your thoughts are in good hands with [the] stone—and the stone can also withstand the greatest worries" (Greiner and Kiem 2019, p. 80–81). At the end of the walk, the path leads past the stone again—whether it is left at the edge of the forest or taken with you again can then be decided. This exercise is originally found under "Putting down luggage" by Luise Reddemann (2016, pp. 64–65).

8.4   Going into the Forest with a Question

Whether in a group setting or in a dyad, one can focus on a specific concern and take it into the forest. In a therapeutic context, this can be an ongoing conflict, uncertainty about one's own feelings in relation to a question, something undefined but burdensome, or simply something one wants to gain clarity about. Here, too, there is the possibility of connecting this question with a symbol, such as a leaf or a branch, or writing the question down. The difference with this exercise is that the question is carried along and yet also put down. This means that one does not constantly think about it, but lets it work during the forest walk and picks it up afterwards—depending on the setting—in the small group or in the dyad.

8.5   Immersing Yourself in the Forest—with all Your Senses

Forest bathing is about immersing yourself with all your senses.

All you need for this immersion is the decision to engage with it. When you enter the forest, you walk slowly and follow the sounds, smells, what you can see, and let yourself be completely absorbed by the forest. "The key to unlocking the power of the forest is in the five senses. Let nature enter through your ears, eyes, nose, mouth, hands and feet" (Li 2018, p. 118).

The sensory exercises are usually guided as follows:

Find a place where you want to linger for a while and settle down there. You can sit, lie down, or even stand, whatever seems appropriate for you at the moment. We now invite you to arrive here with all your senses:

- What do you hear? Close your eyes and listen to what is perceptible very close by, then try to listen a few meters around you. Now listen to how something reaches your ear from a distance.
- Look at the different greens that surround you. Which green attracts you particularly, which less. Move towards it and let it have an effect on you.

- What smells do you perceive? Maybe you pick up a piece of moss or forest soil, or you take a branch or a piece of resin in your hand and smell it.
- Breathe deeply and take in the freshness. Or yawn really heartily, feel the relaxation that spreads not only in your facial features.
- Touch a tree, feel the bark, the branches, lean against the tree, hug it, as it feels good and right for you at the moment.
- Lie down on the ground and feel what it feels like.
- Feel how you have now arrived at this place with all your senses and how a feeling of joy and serenity can spread.

Li refers to the sixth sense as the feeling of joy and serenity that arises when you take in the "taste of the forest": "Drink in the flavour of the forest and release your sense of joy and calm. This is your sixth sense, a state of mind. Now you have connected with nature. You have crossed the bridge to happiness" (p. 121).

8.6   Exercise Three—Two—One

If the entry into the five senses sometimes doesn't seem so easy, this exercise is very helpful:

Choose a place where you can stand well. Notice how you stand firmly on the ground with both legs, your knees are relaxed, not stretched. Notice how your breath flows calmly and well through you into the ground. Your shoulders are relaxed, the top of your head is directed upwards as if by a golden thread. Your face smiles at you gently and kindly.

Now try to see three things around you, don't judge, just pay attention to what catches your eye.

Then try to hear three sounds.

Finally, feel inside yourself and try to feel three feelings.

After that, focus on two things you see, these can be the same or new.

Focus on two sounds and finally on two feelings.

After that, you see one thing,
hear one sound and
feel one feeling.

When you have completed the exercise, indicate this with a nod of your head.

This exercise can be carried out wonderfully both in the forest and indoors and quickly brings individual patients as well as entire groups into an effortless attention mode of complex mindfulness.

8.7 Being Particularly Attracted by a Green

This exercise takes place in the forest.

Look around: Which different greens appeal to you?

Try to find out which green particularly invites you to linger. Pay attention to what kind of green it is: the pea green of a larch in spring, the fir green or the green of the fern in the shade. Or one of the many different greens of the mosses. Pay attention to your breathing, it is in flow, there is no effort involved in the exercise.

The time frame for this exercise is set at 30 min, after which there is an invitation to express the experience—to paint, make a nature mandala, write or put into music what was experienced—in tones, sounds. It is essential here that the experience is condensed and expressed (see Klempnauer 2017, p. 12).

8.8 Take a Closer Look

A magnifying glass is best suited for this exercise.

It usually takes a little time to get used to it, as it brings with it a completely different viewing habit. The results are always very surprising and astonishing when a huge hole is discovered in a small hazelnut, the perfect cut or the fine hairs of a leaf are admired. No matter what is examined under the magnifying glass, the attention is focused there, condenses, and the aesthetic experience is enjoyed. With paper and pens, the explored can also be drawn or described.

8.9 The Walking Meditation Exercise

Notice your breath. The breath flows. You stand on the ground, barefoot or in shoes you feel the ground. You feel how the weight of your body pulls you down, your arms, your shoulders, you feel how gravity affects you. At the same time, you seem to be connected to the sky above by a thread through your spine and the top of your head, standing upright.

Focus on the ground, how it feels under your toes, then your attention switches to your heels and finally you notice your whole foot on the ground.

Now direct your attention to both feet. It is not about reaching a goal as quickly as possible, but about walking, about the journey.

Slowly raise and lower one leg after the other.

Roll your foot off the ball of your foot or switch and step on your heel first. If your breath catches, pause and try to let your breath flow again.

How does the ground feel? Is your posture upright, a smile on your lips, or is your posture bent, strained? If thoughts come that distract you, smile at them and let them pass by and return to your feet on the ground. Is the ground uneven, full of roots, or soft, is it wet or dry, how do you perceive the ground you are walking on?

Nota bene: It is not important to cover a distance, but to walk: the journey, the walking is the goal.

When you finish this exercise, smile at yourself and end the exercise with a few conscious breaths.

8.10   The Roots in My Life

The following exercise is taken from the book "Wald tut gut" (*The forest does you good*):

Walk slowly through the forest for a while and pay attention to the trees around you. You can also stop and take a closer look at some of the trees. What is the circumference of the tree? How tall is the tree? Estimate how old the tree might be.

Now imagine that trees are similar to an iceberg. A large part of the tree is underground and is actually not visible at all. It is precisely this root network that gives the tree many of the nutrients it needs to grow so big and old. In addition, the tree gets anchoring, stability and grounding from this root network. All factors that are necessary for survival.

Now find a section of the forest where you can stand upright. Spread your legs shoulder-width apart, your hands hanging next to your body. If you like, you can close your eyes. Start again with abdominal breathing [or focus on your breaths, note from the author]. …

Next, direct your attention to the soles of your feet. Imagine that you are absorbing vital nutrients from the forest floor into your body as you inhale. As you exhale, imagine roots growing from the soles of your feet and anchoring in the ground. With each breath, you absorb more nutrients and the roots anchor more firmly and deeply in the ground. Feel inside yourself what it feels like to be grounded and anchored like a giant tree. Do you perhaps feel a sense of strength and security? Stay in this state as long as you like and enjoy the feeling of deep rootedness.

After the above reflection exercise, sit down and think about the following questions: What gives you support in your life? Who or what are the roots of your life that nourish you? Are there roots in your life (family, friends, hobbies, etc.) that you would like to become stronger? If so, what can you do to make them grow stronger? (Greiner and Kiem 2019, p. 181)

The selection of exercises so far has been limited to exercises in the forest or at the edge of the forest. Experience shows that it is not always easy to simply return to everyday life after beautiful experiences in the forest. This is particularly difficult when everyday life takes place far away from access to the forest. Some exercises have already referred to the possibilities of writing—Green Writing— and drawing; a booklet like the "Nature Park Time-Out Compass" can support and be seen as a transfer possibility into everyday life.

Before pointing out the possibility and meaningfulness of moments of remembrance, exercise 11 guides the conscious farewell, leaving the forest. The natural transition from the forest to the edge of the forest and out into the open field or meadow is a good opportunity to consciously make this exit.

8.11 Exiting the Forest

You are now coming to the edge of the forest again, which you can tell by the clearing. Stop and consciously look at this edge: What light do you perceive, are the sounds already changing, what do you see? Now close your eyes for a moment and feel how this stay in the forest was for you. How do you perceive your facial features, your shoulders, your arms and legs, your stomach, …? If you were walking barefoot, how do your feet feel? Feel which emotions are currently within you. Perhaps there is also a feeling of gratitude, special serenity. Maybe you feel this feeling in one part of your body in particular—then put your hand there, breathe consciously a few breaths into your hand and anchor the feeling in this part of your body. Release your hand and open your eyes.

When you step out of the forest, you can say "Thank you, forest" softly or loudly and smile at yourself and the forest in a friendly way.

8.12   The Journey Stick Exercise

Journey sticks are travel sticks that are important in the tradition of the Aborigines. A portable stick is taken along or searched for at the beginning of the forest life and is chronologically provided with small natural objects that are attached to it. This journey stick is a reminder of the escape, thus collecting information about the route taken—where it was dry, where there was water, etc. In the context of the Aborigines in the often very harsh nature of Australia, this is an important method of collecting valuable information. For forest life in our latitudes, it can remind us of the escape and thus of what was experienced where, and is also something that can be taken home. An adaptation option is also to take a large pine cone instead of a stick, to which the individual elements are attached (see Greiner and Kiem 2019, pp. 244–246).

8.13   The Tree Exercise

The following exercises—suitable for the interior—are taken from the book "Leibtherapie" (*Body Therapy*) by Hofer-Moser, which contains an extensive appendix of proven exercise instructions. Hofer-Moser has slightly modified the purely imaginative tree exercise according to Luise Reddemann (see 2016, pp. 62–63):

> I would now like to invite you to the tree exercise.
>
> First, imagine a landscape in which you feel comfortable and where you like to stay. This can, but does not have to, be a real landscape. It can also be an invented landscape. [...]
>
> And imagine a tree somewhere in this landscape that you would like to go to, that may even attract you. [...]
>
> And you imagine that you go to this tree and make contact with it by perhaps touching it or looking at it. Notice its trunk, the shape of its bark, and take in the smell. Then notice how the trunk branches out. The leaves. [...]
>
> You first register all of this and make contact with this tree in this way. [...] And if it is possible for you, you can imagine leaning against the tree and really feeling it. [...]
>
> And if you find the idea pleasant, you can now imagine becoming one with the tree. [...]

And then you can experience as a tree what it means to have roots that branch out in the earth to absorb nourishment from there. Experience what it is like to have leaves that absorb sunlight and convert it into usable energy.

If you don't want to merge with the tree, just look at it. Think about what it means for the tree to have roots that give it support and nourishment, and leaves that absorb sunlight. [...]

And then think about what you want to be nourished with, what you want to be provided with. Is it physical nourishment, emotional nourishment, nourishment for the mind, for your spiritual being? Name it as precisely as possible. [...]

And if you are one with the tree, imagine that you receive the desired nourishment from the earth and the sun.

And if you are not merged with the tree, you can perhaps imagine what it means to receive nourishment from the sun and the earth, because that is also the case for us humans.

Allow yourself the experience that this nourishment is now coming to you from the earth and the sun. [...]

And then feel how what you receive from the sun and the earth connects within you. [...] And that you can live and grow as a result. [...]

And then you separate from your tree again. [...]

And you can decide, if you want, to often return to your tree in order to experience with its help that you are nourished with everything you need. [...]

You can, if you like, promise it that you will come back. Say goodbye to it and thank it for its support. [...]

Then come back to the room with full attention. (Hofer-Moser 2018, p. 274–275).

8.14   The Tree Exercise in Embodiment

Please find a good spot in the room with enough distance from the other participants, align your feet parallel and shoulder-width apart, keep your knees slightly bent and your pelvis in a central position. The upper body is relaxed and slightly upright, so that you may feel a flexible firmness in the lower body and legs and a lightness in the upper body. The arms hang down completely relaxed at first.

Now imagine what it would be like to stand there as a "healthy, strong tree" with roots that reach deep into the earth and provide both sufficient stability in strong storms and adequate water intake with all the nutrients needed. [...]

And now imagine how this strong, healthy trunk divides into branches and twigs with leaves that can absorb the energy of the sun, the energy that can transform the nutrients taken in through the roots into everything the tree needs to live and grow, both physically, emotionally, mentally and spiritually.

And now you may allow your arms and hands to position themselves in the room as they correspond to your inner image of the tree you are embodying. […] Just experiment with the positions until it feels roughly right "from the inside".

And when you have found your expression as a tree, you can also ask yourself *which tree* you are embodying. Is it a deciduous tree or a conifer? […] And which conifer or deciduous tree exactly? […] In which landscape is this tree located? […] And is it standing on its own, with a few companions, or in a forest? […] What season is it? […] Can you perhaps also feel how a gentle wind plays with your leaves and branches? […] You may even want to try what it is like when a stronger wind blows or even a storm, and the strong roots and healthy trunk can prove themselves. […]

And perhaps animals will also come to visit: birds, squirrels, various insects, etc., whatever feels good and right to you from all these ideas. […]

At the end, I ask you to switch back to your "animal existence", to retract your "roots", to say goodbye to "your" tree and to move slowly through the room, stretching and stretching, […] whatever you need to be fully present again. (Hofer-Moser 2018, p. 275–276)

In practice, it has proven useful in these two exercises to invite participants to creative expression—whether in painting or writing—immediately after the exercise, before exchanging ideas in pairs or in a group setting. Paper of different sizes and artists' crayons should be provided. Another option is to display the resulting pictures and texts and view them as in a silent exhibition tour before exchanging ideas.

The Forest on the Prescription

"Forest prescription" can promote lifestyle changes in cases of depression. A depression treatment initially requires a medical assessment. Based on this, an integrative bundle of measures is necessary.

"The basic structure in the background of such a bundle of measures is provided in integrative therapy by the consistent orientation to the therapy process (processual diagnostics) and the concept of the 'Four Paths of Healing and Encouragement '" (Reichel et al. 2018, p. 43–44).

Furthermore, it requires—but not necessarily in this order:

- A committed relationship offer that can enable the patient to feel emotions again and accept them. Reliable acceptance by the therapist enables corrective experiences.
- An intermittent focal psychotherapy that includes, among other things, work on changing negative cognitions, negative emotions ("learned helplessness") and "will empowerment".
- Network therapeutic measures to change relationships in the family, circle of friends, neighborhood, colleagues, to experience community and solidarity […] and possibly the acquisition of a pet.
- Body, movement and sports therapeutic measures including activities related to nature.
- Educational and creative therapeutic measures including strengthening the motivation for work ability and professional development (training, etc.).

© The Author(s), under exclusive license to Springer Fachmedien Wiesbaden GmbH, part of Springer Nature 2023
A. Polz-Watzenig, *The Healing Effect of the Forest in Integrative Therapy*,
Springer essentials, https://doi.org/10.1007/978-3-658-41643-0_9

- A critical reflection of one's own illness in society. (see p. 43–44)

Experience shows that recipes for this lifestyle change can be "prescribed". This remedy can include, for example, regarding forest experiences:

- Go into the forest twice a day for 20–30 min and walk briskly there so that you don't get out of breath.
- Look at a tree or plant in the forest or at the edge of the forest for 10 min every day, which caught your attention. (This often requires a kind of "dry training", a joint practice in the therapy session: how do I sit, how do I breathe, how can I practice so that my thoughts don't always distract me, etc.).
- In this context, special attention should be paid to the Three-two-one exercise.

These recipes can be incorporated into the therapy session over and over again and be prescribed anew. Sometimes it is also necessary to ask what the patient needs in order for the recipe to be redeemable, if someone, for example, does not want to go into the forest alone. Then solutions can be worked out together. Who can be asked if they want to come along? Is there perhaps a Nordic walking group that one could join? The hurdles should not be too big and must be feasible for the patient. It is advisable for the therapist to ask how the recipe redemption worked or whether the recipe has already been redeemed.

In the overview of measures to be taken in the treatment of depression, one aspect is the critical reflection of the disease in society. It is advisable for the therapist to always keep the perspective of ecopsychosomatics in mind.

Environmental destruction makes people sick, stress makes people sick, alienation from nature makes people sick; the constant overburdening, the noise that people are often involuntarily exposed to, the performance requirements of a digitized economy—all this and much more can make people sick.

On the other hand, there is much that gives hope and confidence: people who are committed to preserving nature and fighting climate change, the "Fridays for Future" movement and one or the other "Urban Gardening" movement in city districts full of asphalt and concrete. People who are engaged experience both their own effectiveness and a feeling of belonging and solidarity. Experiencing and engaging oneself in corrective ecological action can be a possibility within the integrative bundle of measures, which can thus be effective in a double sense in terms of sustainability.

9.1   The Forest in the Group Therapy Setting

In both individual and group therapy settings, it is important to clarify whether the experience of the forest is "usable". It is necessary to clarify in advance whether there are physical restrictions, mobility impairments, grass, pollen or fungus spore allergies, or allergic reactions to insect bites to consider. It is also important to clarify whether the therapist is familiar with the route, the dyad or group can be undisturbed there, the path is easily accessible for everyone, or if it is blocked by fallen trees after a storm. In other words, the therapist needs some preparation time, both alone and with and for the group (see Ellerbrock and Petzold 2019, pp. 752–755).

When inviting the group, it is important to make sure that appropriate clothing, change of clothes, rain protection, sunscreen in summer, and a water bottle are packed. Before going into the forest, it is good to get to know each other as a group and to establish common rules—as a group with each other, but also for behavior in the forest.

It requires—even in the forest—protected spaces as a group that can be used for exchange with each other, i.e. undisturbed spaces.

It is important to ensure that the participants have enough time for themselves as well as being able to get into creative expression and that the communication of the expression takes place in exchange—in dyads, triads, small groups or in the plenary session.

Practicing mindfulness exercises together in the forest and perceiving that the forest can act as a companion along one's own life questions usually leads to great intensity and density in the groups. There is also the possibility of combining shared moments, e.g. eating together, with mindfulness exercises; these are also elements that are often and gladly transferred into everyday life and can contribute to deceleration and self-care.

The four paths of healing and encouragement described in Integrative Therapy

- "Bewusstseinsarbeit" (Fostering of awareness) and finding meaning,
- Post -socialization and basic trust,
- Activation of experience and personality development, and
- Experience of solidarity, multiperspectivity and engagement

can be consciously experienced by each participant with the help of the forest experience in the group and transferred sustainably into personal everyday life through joint reflection (see Krüskemper 2019, pp. 621–623).

Critical Reflection—Limitations

10

Finally, with all the desire for movement "Back to nature", it should be noted that it is important to consider that the inclusion of the forest experience in therapeutic practice may not be suitable and helpful for all patients.

For patients whose childhood was meagre and/or who had to work a lot—also in the forest—it is possible that the forest cannot primarily be experienced as a place of relaxation, because it has not been known in this way so far.

There may have been traumatic experiences in the forest; the forest can be a place of fear, which is deeply rejected, for example due to the memory of forestry accidents or assaults in the forest.

In the event that allergies or insect or tick phobias exist, the forest experience will also be contraindicated (for the time being).

The fact that someone simply does not appreciate the forest or nature is also a sufficient reason to mention. As a rule, it is quite useful in this as well as in all other examples mentioned to get to the bottom of the rejecting attitude in the course of therapy.

Another limit arises when the therapist herself does not feel comfortable in the forest or is worried that she cannot guide this forest experience. In such a case, there is the possibility of working with colleagues from the field of forest pedagogy. In the forest experience, this is generally a well-implementable option, but in the area of therapeutic work, attention must be paid to the distribution of roles and tasks, and the question remains open as to how much one's own insecurity can be overcome and whether the forest experience can then form a suitable framework at all.

Intersubjectivity and co-response in the process of integrative therapy require authenticity in addition to empathy.

A. Polz-Watzenig, *The Healing Effect of the Forest in Integrative Therapy*, Springer essentials, https://doi.org/10.1007/978-3-658-41643-0_10

What you can take away from this *essential*

- The healing effect of the forest can be made accessible to patients as an immediate resource with simple exercises.
- The use of the exercises presented here opens up new development potential in therapeutic work.
- The forest experience is well suited as a self-care option for therapists.
- The attitude of complex mindfulness enables a deeper ecological understanding.
- When looking at the healing effect of the forest, eco-philosophy, eco-philia and mindful self-care can be combined as resources.

References

Carrington, D. (2019). Two-hour ‚dose‘ of nature significantly boosts health – study. Researchers say simply sitting and enjoying the peace has mental and physical benefits. *The Guardian.* https://www.theguardian.com/environment/2019/jun/13/two-hour-dose-nature-weekly-boosts-health-study-finds Accessed: August 2, 2019.

Ellerbrock, B., & Petzold, H. G. (2019). Die Heilkraft des Waldes, Klinische Naturtherapie, erlebnisorientierte Psychotherapie und die Ökopsychosomatik der Waldlandschaft. In H. G. Petzold, B. Ellerbrock & R. Hömberg (Eds.), Die Neuen Naturtherapien. Handbuch der Garten-, Landschafts-, Wald- und Tiergestützten Therapie. Band I; Grundlagen Garten- und Landschaftstherapie (pp. 741–762). Bielefeld: Aisthesis Verlag.

Gemoll, W. (1954). Griechisch-deutsches Schul- und Handwörterbuch (9. Auflage). München: G. Freytag Verlag.

Greiner, K., & Kiem, M. (2019). *Wald tut gut!: Stress abbauen, Wohlbefinden und Gesundheit stärken.* Aarau: AT-Verlag.

Haluza, D. (2019). Heilsames Eintauchen ins Grün. Gehirn und Geist, 8, 12–19.

Hofer-Moser, O. (2018). Leibtherapie. Eine neue Perspektive auf Körper und Seele. Gießen: Psychosozial-Verlag.

Hömberg, R., & Petzold, H. G. (2019). Ökopsychosomatik und ökologische Neurowissenschaften. Integrative Perspektiven für die „Neuen Naturtherapien" und das Engagement „Pro natura!". In H. G. Petzold, B. Ellerbrock & R. Hömberg (Hrsg.), Die Neuen Naturtherapien. Handbuch der Garten-, Landschafts-, Wald- und Tiergestützten Therapie. Band I; Grundlagen Garten- und Landschaftstherapie (S. 257–272). Bielefeld: Aisthesis Verlag.

Klempnauer, E. (19/2017). Green Writing – Schreiben in der Natur und von Naturerfahrungen – Ein integrativer Ansatz kreativen und biographischen Schreibens. FPI-Publikationen. https://www.fpi-publikation.de/downloads/?doc=sonstiges_klempnauer-green-writing-schreiben-in-der-natur-naturerfahrungen-biographisch-gruene-text-19-2017.pdf Accessed: April 28, 2020.

Krüskemper, S. (2019). Integrative Gartentherapie in der Arbeit mit biographisch belasteten Menschen. In H. G. Petzold, B. Ellerbrock & R. Hömberg (Hrsg.), Die Neuen Naturtherapien. Handbuch der Garten-, Landschafts-, Wald- und Tiergestützten Therapie. Band I; Grundlagen Garten- und Landschaftstherapie (S. 611–688). Bielefeld: Aisthesis Verlag.

Leitner, A. (2010). *Handbuch der Integrativen Therapie.* Wien: Springer.

Li, Q. (2018). *Shinrin-Yoku: The Art and Science of Forest – Bathing, How Trees Can Help You Find Health and Happiness.* London: Penguin Random House UK.

Li, Q. (2019). Die Heilkraft des Waldes – Der Beitrag der Waldmedizin zur Naturtherapie. In: H. G. Petzold, B. Ellerbrock, & R. Hömberg (Hrsg.), Die Neuen Naturtherapien. Handbuch der Garten-, Landschafts-, Wald- und Tiergestützten Therapie. Band I; Grundlagen Garten- und Landschaftstherapie (S. 273–289). Bielefeld: Aisthesis Verlag.

Macfarlane, R. (2017). *The Wild Places.* London: Granta Books.

Moser, M., & Thoma, E. (2014). *Die sanfte Medizin der Bäume, Gesund leben mit altem und neuem Wissen.* Salzburg: Servus Verlag.

Osten, P. (2000). *Die Anamnese in der Psychotherapie* (2nd Ed.). München: E. Reinhardt Verlag.

Petzold, H. G. (2003). *Integrative Therapie. Modelle, Theorien & Methoden einer schulenübergreifenden Psychotherapie* (3Bde.) (2. überarbeitete und erweiterte Aufl.). Paderborn: Junfermann Verlag.

Petzold, H. G. (2015). *Green Meditation – Ruhe, Kraft, Lebensfreude.* FPI-Publikationen. https://www.fpi-publikation.de/polyloge/alle-ausgaben/05-2015-petzold-hilarion-g-2015b-green-meditation-ruhe-kraft-lebensfreude.html Accessed: April 28, 2020.

Petzold, H. G., Orth, I., & Sieper, J. (2016). *„14 plus 3" – Wege des Integrierens und Einflussfaktoren im Entwicklungsgeschehen: Belastungs-, Schutz-, Resilienzfaktoren bzw. -prozesse und die Wirk- und Heilfaktoren/-prozesse der Integrativen Therapie.* Handout. Hückeswagen: Europäische Akademie für biopsychosoziale Gesundheit.

Petzold, H. G., Ellerbrock B., & Hömberg, R. (2019). *Die „Neuen Naturtherapien": Formen, Konzepte, Perspektiven – eine Übersicht.* In H. G. Petzold, B. Ellerbrock & R. Hömberg (Hrsg.), Die Neuen Naturtherapien. Handbuch der Garten-, Landschafts-, Wald- und Tiergestützten Therapie. Band I; Grundlagen Garten- und Landschaftstherapie (S. 31–70). Bielefeld: Aisthesis Verlag.

Petzold, H. G., Moser, S. B., & Orth, I. (2019). *Euthyme Therapie – Heilkunst und Gesundheitsförderung in asklepiadischer Tradition: Ein integrativer und behavioraler Behandlungsansatz „multipler Stimulierung" und „Lebensstilveränderung".* In H. G. Petzold, B. Ellerbrock & R. Hömberg (Hrsg.), Die Neuen Naturtherapien. Handbuch der Garten-, Landschafts-, Wald- und Tiergestützten Therapie. Band I; Grundlagen Garten- und Landschaftstherapie (S. 189–256). Bielefeld: Aisthesis Verlag.

Petzold, H. G., & Orth-Petzold, S. (2019). Naturentfremdung, bedrohte Ökologisation, Internetsucht – psychotherapeutische und ökopsychosomatische Perspektiven. POLYLOGE – Eine Internetzeitschrift für „Integrative Therapie." https://www.fpi-publikation.de/downloads/?doc=polyloge_petzold-orth-petzold-2018a-naturentfremdung-bedrohte-oekologisation-internetsucht-polyloge-06-2019.pdf Accessed: April 28, 2020.

Pollack, K. (2019). Zeitgeist. Neurologe Lalouschek: Burnout wird von vielen Seiten missbraucht. Interview, 29. Mai 2019. Der Standard. https://www.derstandard.at/story/200010 2894966/neurologe-lalouschek-burnout-wird-von-vielen-missbraucht Accessed: August 2, 2019.

Polz-Watzenig, A. (2019). *Die heilsame Wirkung des Waldes aus Sicht der Integrativen Therapie.* Master-Thesis zur Erlangung des akademischen Grades Master of Science im Universitätslehrgang Psychotherapie – Integrative Therapie. Donau-Universität Krems.

Reddemann, L. (2016a). Imagination als heilsame Kraft. Ressourcen und Mitgefühl in der Behandlung von Traumafolgen (19. Aufl.). Stuttgart: Klett-Cotta.

Reichel, R., Brunner, F., Enk, B., Jobst, A., & Magdowski, R. (2018). Depression aus Sicht der Integrativen Therapie. Resonanzen – E-Journal für biopsychosoziale Dialoge in Psychosomatischer Medizin, Psychotherapie, Supervision und Beratung. www.resonanzen-journal.org Accessed: August 10, 2019.

Schmitz, H. (2015). *Der Leib, der Raum und die Gefühle.* Bielefeld: Aisthesis Verlag.

Wohlleben, P. (2016). *Der Wald. Eine Entdeckungsreise.* München: Heyne Verlag.

Printed in the United States
by Baker & Taylor Publisher Services